NOTES FOR THE READER

This book uses both imperial, metric or US cup measurements. Follow the same units
of measurement throughout; do not mix metric and imperial. All spoon measurements
are level; teaspoons are assumed to be 15ml. Unless otherwise stated, milk is
assumed to be full fat, individual vegetables such as potatoes are medium, and
pepper is freshly ground black pepper. Recipes using raw or very lightly cooked eggs
should be avoided by infants, the elderly, pregnant women, convalescents and
anyone suffering from an illness. The times given are an approximate guide only.
Preparation times differ according to the techniques used by different people and the
cooking times may also vary from those given.

CONTENTS

introduction 4

 a little something to start

 table for two

 a fine finish

INTRODUCTION

Cooking for someone else, whether a friend, partner, or flat mate, is one of the **best reasons** to get into the kitchen. The **joy** of cooking for another person is that the process of cooking, and the meal itself, can become anything you want. Cooking during the week can be a **relaxing** and very rewarding end to the day, especially as the cook decides the menu!

The whole point of cooking for friends or partners is to be comfortable. Whether you are cooking for a **special occasion**, or preparing a quick and easy meal at the end of a busy day, making a meal shouldn't be a drag. It is far better to choose a simpler dish, done to **perfection**, than to attempt an overcomplicated meal with less than perfect results.

Cooking for Two will reveal the secret to **fantastic** and **hassle-free** cuisine. Think Broiled Lemon Salmon, followed by Individual Chocolate Desserts; simplicity and decadence all in the same meal. It's not all about how many hours you slaved over the stove. It's about how tasty the dish is.

A classic dish such as Spaghetti and Meatballs is **delicious** if you take a little time to make it, and the result will be far better than opening a jar of sauce. Other dishes to **impress** your eating companion include Pork in White Wine and Olive Sauce, or sumptuous Crunchy Beef with Hot Citrus Sauce. And with a choice of several **luscious** desserts you won't be able to resist the third course!

What better **reward** at the end of the day than a delicious meal, made all the tastier because you are cooking for someone else. And remember, the meal is for you too, so relax and **enjoy**!

A LITTLE *something to* START

First impressions are always important, and these dishes

are guaranteed to make an impact as well as being so

simple to make! Try the fantastic *Smoked Salmon,*

Asparagus & Avocado Salad or a delicious *Rösti*.

A classic *Red Onion Tomato & Herb Salad* is always a hit,

and you'll be dying to feast your senses on flavorful

Crispy Roast Asparagus.

CRISPY ROAST ASPARAGUS

♥♥♥   2   serves 2   5 mins   10-15 mins
extremely
easy

ingredients

8 asparagus stalks

1 tbsp extra virgin olive oil

½ tsp coarse sea salt

1 tbsp grated Parmesan cheese,
  to serve

Preheat the oven to 400°F/200°C.

Choose asparagus stalks of similar widths. Trim the base of the stalks so that all the stems are approximately the same length.

Arrange the asparagus in a single layer on a cookie sheet. Drizzle with olive oil and sprinkle with salt.

Place the cookie sheet in the oven and bake for 10–15 minutes, turning once. Remove from the oven, transfer to an attractive dish, and serve immediately, sprinkled with the grated Parmesan.

SMOKED SALMON, ASPARAGUS & AVOCADO SALAD

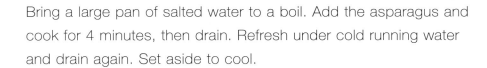

♥♥♥   very easy |❨2❩| serves 2   ◔ 15 mins   ◷ 5 mins

ingredients

3½ oz/100 g fresh asparagus spears

1 medium ripe avocado

½ tbsp lemon juice

large handful fresh arugula leaves

4 oz/110 g smoked salmon slices

1 small red onion, finely sliced

½ tbsp chopped fresh flatleaf parsley

½ tbsp chopped fresh chives

DRESSING

1 garlic clove, chopped

4 tbsp extra-virgin olive oil

2 tbsp white wine vinegar

1 tbsp lemon juice

pinch of sugar

1 tsp mustard

GARNISH

sprigs of fresh flatleaf parsley

wedges of lemon

fresh whole-wheat bread, to serve

Bring a large pan of salted water to a boil. Add the asparagus and cook for 4 minutes, then drain. Refresh under cold running water and drain again. Set aside to cool.

To make the dressing, combine all the ingredients in a small bowl and stir together well. Cut the avocado in half lengthwise, then remove and discard the pit and skin. Cut the flesh into bite-size pieces and brush with lemon juice to prevent discoloration.

To assemble the salad, arrange the arugula on individual serving plates and top with the asparagus and avocado. Cut the smoked salmon into strips and scatter over the top of the salad, then scatter over the onion and herbs. Drizzle over the dressing, then garnish with fresh parsley sprigs and lemon wedges. Serve with fresh whole-wheat bread.

RED ONION, TOMATO & HERB SALAD

♥♥♥ | 🍴②🍴 | 🥄 | 🕐
extremely easy | serves 2 | 10 mins | 20 mins to chill

ingredients

1 lb/450 g tomatoes, sliced thinly

½ tbsp sugar, optional

salt and pepper

1 small red onion, sliced thinly
into rings

large handful coarsely chopped
fresh herbs

DRESSING

2–4 tbsp vegetable oil

2 tbsp red wine vinegar or
fruit vinegar

Arrange the tomato slices in a shallow bowl. Sprinkle with sugar (if using), salt, and pepper.

Separate the onion slices into rings and sprinkle them over the tomatoes. Sprinkle the herbs over the top. Any fresh herbs that are in season can be used—for example, tarragon, sorrel, cilantro, or basil.

Place the dressing ingredients in a jar with a screw-top lid. Shake well. Pour the dressing over the salad and mix gently.

Cover with plastic wrap and chill for 20 minutes. Remove the salad from the refrigerator 5 minutes before serving, unwrap the dish, and stir gently before setting out on the table.

TABLE *for* TWO

The recipes in this main section are so good you may not want to share them! Take a look at *Broiled Lemon Salmon* for pure sophistication. *Penne with Hot Pepper Broccoli* has a kick, and *Pan-braised Chicken* will have your guest coming back for more. There is a range of vegetable, fish, and meat dishes to delight all tastes.

PAN-BRAISED CHICKEN

♥♥♥ very easy   serves 2   10 mins   60 mins

ingredients

2 tbsp olive oil

2 chicken leg quarters

1 small onion, chopped roughly

4 tomatoes, diced

3 tbsp diced red bell pepper

1 small zucchini, sliced thinly
  or diced

8 white mushrooms, sliced thinly

1 garlic clove, crushed

  1 small fresh chili, seeded and
  diced or ½ tsp chili flakes (optional)

1 tsp dried oregano or basil

salt and pepper

scant 1 cup chicken stock

Heat the oil over high heat in a large skillet. Sauté the chicken for about 5 minutes, skin side down, until golden brown. Turn and brown the second side.

Add the onion, tomatoes, bell pepper, zucchini, mushrooms, garlic, and chili or chili flakes, if using. Sprinkle in the herbs and season to taste with salt and pepper. Mix well.

Pour in the stock, bring to a boil, then reduce the heat so that the liquid is just simmering. Cover the skillet and cook for 45 minutes, turning the chicken occasionally.

Transfer the chicken to a serving dish and keep it warm in a low oven. Increase the heat to high and boil the sauce hard so that it thickens and reduces. Spoon it over the chicken and serve.

BROILED MEXICAN CHICKEN

♥♥♥ very easy | serves 2 | 10 mins + 30 mins to chill | 15 mins

ingredients

*2 skinless, boneless chicken
  breast portions*

juice of 1 lemon

2 tbsp olive oil

1 small onion, sliced thinly

*1 small red bell pepper, seeded and
  sliced thinly*

*1 small green bell pepper, seeded
  and sliced thinly*

1 tsp chili powder

½ tsp black pepper

SERVING SUGGESTIONS

sour cream

guacamole

refried beans

grated cheese

shredded lettuce

jalapeño chilies

salsa

tortillas, rice, or baked potato

Cut each chicken portion into 4 strips lengthwise. Place in a dish, sprinkle with lemon juice, mix, cover, and chill for 30 minutes.

Heat 1 tablespoonful of olive oil on high on a heavy griddle and toss on the onion and bell peppers. Cook over medium heat for 3 minutes, then sprinkle with chili powder, and mix well. Cook for 2 minutes more, then transfer to a warm serving dish.

Remove the chicken from the refrigerator and discard the lemon juice. Sprinkle with black pepper. Heat the remaining olive oil over high heat on the griddle and toss on the chicken. Cook, stirring frequently, for about 5 minutes.

Return the vegetables to the pan and cook for 3–4 minutes to combine the flavors.

Serve the chicken and vegetables immediately, accompanied by any or all of the serving suggestions listed above.

CHILI CON CARNE

♥♥♥   🍴❷🍴   ⌣   🕐

very easy   serves 2   10 mins   60 mins

ingredients

1 tbsp oil

1 small onion, chopped coarsely

1 or 2 garlic cloves, chopped coarsely

1 green bell pepper, seeded and diced

2 cups ground beef

1 heaping tsp chili powder

*14 oz/400 g canned chopped
    tomatoes*

½ tsp salt, optional

*14 oz/400 g canned kidney beans,
    drained and rinsed*

SERVING SUGGESTIONS

grated cheese

shredded lettuce and tomatoes

guacamole

jalapeño chilies

rice, tortillas or bread

Heat the oil over low heat in a shallow skillet. Stir in the onion, garlic, and green bell pepper and cook gently for 5 minutes.

Add the beef and stir well. Turn up the heat to high and cook for 5 minutes, stirring occasionally. Spoon off any excess fat. Sprinkle in the chili powder and mix well. Continue cooking for 2–3 minutes. Stir in the tomatoes, reduce the heat, cover, and cook gently for at least 30 minutes. You may need to add more tomatoes or a little water or beef stock if it starts to dry out.

Check for seasoning and stir in the salt if needed. Add more chili powder to taste, but be careful not to overdo it. Add the drained kidney beans to the chili mixture 10–15 minutes before the end of the cooking time so that they heat through with the meat and spices.

Serve with any of the accompaniments listed above.

CRUNCHY BEEF WITH HOT CITRUS SAUCE

♥♥♥ very easy
🍴② serves 2
⏲ 5 mins + 15 mins to marinate
🕐 10 mins

ingredients

MARINADE

1 tsp dark soy sauce

1 tsp fish sauce

1 garlic clove, crushed

oil, for deep-frying

8 oz/225 g steak, cut into thin strips

2 tbsp cornstarch

CITRUS SAUCE

6 tbsp brown sugar

1 tsp cornstarch

4 tbsp dark soy sauce

4 tbsp rice wine

grated rind and juice of 1 orange

SERVING SUGGESTIONS

broccoli or bok choy, stir-fried with garlic

spring rolls or rice

Combine the soy sauce, fish sauce, and garlic in a mixing bowl. Add the strips of meat, stir to coat, cover, and chill 15 minutes.

Heat enough oil in a wok or large skillet to deep-fry the meat. Remove the meat, drain off the marinade, and toss the meat in cornstarch. Shake off any excess. Drop the strips of meat into the hot oil and cook quickly for 1–2 minutes, or until golden brown. Remove with a slotted spoon and drain on paper towels.

To make the sauce, combine the brown sugar and cornstarch in a small pan. Stir in the soy sauce, rice wine, and orange juice. Bring to a boil, then simmer gently for 2 minutes, stirring constantly.

Return the beef and 1 tablespoon of oil to the wok or skillet. Sprinkle in the orange rind. Stir quickly to reheat.

Transfer the beef to a serving dish and pour the sauce over it. Serve immediately with one or two of the other dishes suggested.

MEATBALLS & SPAGHETTI

easy | serves 2 | 10 mins + 20 mins to make tomato sauce | 30 mins

ingredients

1 thick slice crustless white bread

water, for soaking

1 quantity tomato sauce

2 cups ground beef

1 egg

1 tsp chopped fresh parsley

1 tsp chopped fresh basil

1 garlic clove, finely chopped

½ tsp salt

6 oz/175 g dried spaghetti

freshly grated Parmesan cheese,
   to serve

Put the bread in a shallow dish and add water just to cover. After 5 minutes, drain, and squeeze the bread to remove all the liquid.

Heat the tomato sauce in a large pan over medium heat. Reduce the heat and simmer gently.

Mix the bread, beef, egg, herbs, garlic, and salt by hand in a large bowl. Roll small pieces of the meat mixture into balls. Drop the meatballs into the tomato sauce, cover the pan, and cook over medium heat for 30 minutes.

Meanwhile, cook the spaghetti in plenty of boiling water for 10 minutes, or until al dente. Drain, rinse, and drain again.

Turn the spaghetti into a large shallow serving bowl. Arrange the meatballs and sauce on top. Sprinkle 2 tablespoons of freshly grated Parmesan cheese over the top and serve more cheese in a bowl on the side.

LAMB CURRY

❤❤	🍽②🍴	🥄	🕐
easy	serves 2	10 mins	1-2 hrs

ingredients

2 tbsp oil or ghee

1 onion, chopped

1 garlic clove, chopped

½ inch/1 cm piece fresh ginger root,
  peeled and chopped

1 tsp paprika

½ tsp cayenne pepper

½ tsp ground cumin

½ tsp ground coriander

½ tsp garam masala

1 lb/450 g boneless lamb, cubed

3 small tomatoes

½ tsp salt

¼ cup plain yogurt

TO SERVE

rice or nan

mango chutney or pickle

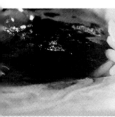

Heat the oil or ghee in a shallow pan over medium heat. Add the onions and garlic and cook until browned.

Add the ginger and continue cooking, stirring constantly, for 2 minutes more. Add the other spices and mix well. Reduce the heat and cook gently for 3 minutes.

Stir the lamb into the spice mixture and cook over medium heat until the meat is sealed all over.

Peel and chop the tomatoes. Add to the meat with the salt and yogurt. Stir well to blend, bring to a boil, then reduce the heat, and simmer, covered, until the meat is tender. This will take 1–1½ hours depending on the size of the lamb cubes and the depth of the pan.

Turn the curry into a serving dish and offer rice, nan, chutney, or pickle as accompaniments

BROILED LEMON SALMON

❤❤❤ extremely easy

serves 2

5 mins

15 mins

ingredients

4 oz/115 g salmon fillet or steak

juice of ½ lemon

1 tbsp butter, diced

salt and pepper

fresh parsley or dill, to garnish

Preheat the broiler to high.

Place the salmon fillet or steak on a rack over the broiler pan. Sprinkle lemon juice over the fish, dot with butter, and season with salt and pepper.

Cook for 10–15 minutes (or until the fish is firm and flakes when checked with a fork), turning once. Cooking time will vary depending on the thickness of the fillet.

Transfer to a serving dish and arrange sprigs of fresh herbs around the fish to garnish.

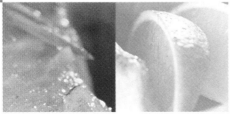

SWEET & SOUR GINGER FISH

❤❤ | 🍽②🍴 | ⏱ | 🕐

easy | serves 2 | 10 mins | 25 mins

ingredients

2 large white fish fillets, skinned

1 egg, beaten

3 heaping tbsp all-purpose flour

oil for deep-frying

2 tbsp butter

1 green bell pepper, seeded and diced

5 scallions, thinly sliced

SAUCE

2 tsp cornstarch

1 tsp sugar

2 tsp wine vinegar

3 tsp sweet sherry

1¼ cups water

1 tbsp tomato paste

6 pieces preserved ginger, diced

1 tbsp ginger syrup

rice and salad, to serve

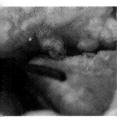

Cut the fish into large, bite-size pieces. Dip the pieces in the egg, then drain, and dredge in flour. Heat the oil and fry the fish pieces quickly for 3–4 minutes, or until they are golden brown. Drain on a dish lined with paper towels.

Melt the butter in a small skillet and cook the green bell pepper and scallions over medium heat for 5 minutes to soften.

Preheat the oven to 300°F/150°C.

To make the sauce, mix the cornstarch and sugar in a small bowl. Stirring constantly, add the vinegar and sherry, then gradually add the water and tomato paste. Finally, mix in the ginger pieces and syrup.

Arrange the fish in a shallow ovenproof dish. Pour the sauce over it and mix gently. Bake for 15 minutes.

Serve the fish with rice and mixed salad greens.

PENNE WITH HOT PEPPER BROCCOLI

❤❤❤   very easy

🍽 ②   serves 2

🕐   5 mins

🕐   15 mins

ingredients

1½ cups dried penne, ziti or other
   large macaroni
1 small head fresh broccoli,
   cut into florets
4 tbsp olive oil
2 garlic cloves, slivered
1 small fresh chili, seeded and
   cut into thin strips, or 1 tsp dried
   chili flakes
TO SERVE
1 tbsp chopped fresh basil
freshly grated Parmesan cheese

Cook the penne in a large pan of boiling salted water for
10 minutes, or until it is al dente. Drain, rinse with cold water,
and drain again. Return to the pan.

Meanwhile, cook the broccoli in a large pan of boiling salted
water for 6–8 minutes. It should be only just tender. Remove
from the heat, drain, rinse with cold water, and drain again.

Heat the oil in a large skillet over high heat until it is sizzling.
Add the garlic and fresh chili or chili flakes and cook for 1 minute.
Add the broccoli and mix well. Reduce the heat to medium and
cook for 2 minutes more to heat through.

Pour the broccoli and garlic mixture over the penne and mix well.
Turn into a large serving dish and sprinkle with basil and cheese.

A *fine* FINISH

For the grand finale, you can be as adventurous as you

wish. *Raspberry Brûlées* are so quick to make and

Individual Chocolate Desserts look very professional.

Why not try a delicious smoothie made with

strawberries and cream? With recipes this easy and

eye-catching, you might feel like you're cheating!

INDIVIDUAL CHOCOLATE DESSERTS

easy   serves 2   10-15 mins   50 mins

ingredients

DESSERTS

½ cup superfine sugar

3 eggs

½ cup all-purpose flour

½ cup unsweetened cocoa

scant ½ cup unsalted butter, melted,
plus extra for greasing

3½ oz/100 g semisweet chocolate,
melted

CHOCOLATE SAUCE

2 tbsp unsalted butter

3½ oz/100 g semisweet chocolate

5 tbsp water

1 tbsp superfine sugar

1 tbsp coffee-flavored liqueur, such
as Kahlua

coffee beans, to decorate

To make four desserts, put the sugar and eggs into a heatproof bowl and place over a pan of simmering water. Whisk for about 10 minutes until frothy. Remove the bowl from the heat and fold in the flour and cocoa. Fold in the butter, then the chocolate. Mix well. Grease 4 small heatproof bowls with butter. Spoon the mixture into the bowls and cover with waxed paper. Top with foil and secure with string. Place the desserts in a large pan filled with enough simmering water to reach halfway up the sides of the bowls. Steam for about 40 minutes, or until cooked through.

About 2–3 minutes before the end of the cooking time, make the sauce. Put the butter, chocolate, water, and sugar into a small pan and warm over low heat, stirring constantly, until melted together. Stir in the liqueur.

Remove the desserts from the heat, turn out into serving dishes, and pour over the sauce. Decorate with coffee beans and serve.

RASPBERRY BRÛLÉES

♥♥♥   🍴②   ☉   🕐

very easy   serves 2   10 mins   7-8 mins

ingredients

4¹⁄₂ oz/125 g raspberries

¹⁄₂ tbsp lemon juice

1 tbsp raspberry preserve

¹⁄₄ cup crème fraîche or mascarpone

¹⁄₄ cup heavy cream, lightly whipped

¹⁄₂ tbsp vanilla extract

3 tbsp superfine sugar

whole raspberries, to decorate

Put the raspberries and lemon juice into a pan and stir over low heat for about 5 minutes until they start to soften. Remove from the heat, stir in the preserve, then divide between 2 ramekins.

Preheat the broiler to hot. In a bowl, mix together the crème fraîche, cream, and vanilla. Spoon the mixture over the raspberries and level the surfaces. Sprinkle the superfine sugar over the top, allowing 1¹⁄₂ tablespoons per ramekin. Cook under the preheated broiler, as close to the flames or element as possible, for 2–3 minutes, until the sugar caramelizes. Remove from the broiler, decorate with whole raspberries, and serve immediately. Alternatively, to serve chilled, let cool to room temperature, then cover with plastic wrap and place in the refrigerator to chill for 3–4 hours.

BUCK'S FIZZ

❤❤❤
very easy

🍴②🔪
serves 2

🥄
0 mins

🕐
0 mins

ingredients

4 measures chilled champagne

4 measures chilled orange juice

Pour half the champagne into each chilled champagne flute, then pour in the orange juice.

STRAWBERRIES & CREAM

Put the strawberries, cream, milk, and sugar into a food processor and process until smooth.

Pour into glasses, decorate with sprigs of fresh mint, and serve.

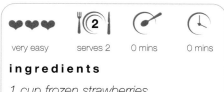

| very easy | serves 2 | 0 mins | 0 mins |

ingredients

1 cup frozen strawberries

generous ⅓ cup light cream

generous ¾ cup cold whole milk

1 tbsp superfine sugar

TO DECORATE

sprigs of fresh mint